Journey with the Wind

Journey with the Wind

For Bill and Charmaine Nichols
Thank you for your
contributions at the
Mountain Missions Conference.
Pearl
July 2007

POETRY
And Short Stories

By

Evelyn Pearl (Carpenter) Anderson

Evelyn Pearl Anderson

Library of Congress Control Number: 2006930990

ISBN-10: 0-9629142-9-0
ISBN-13: 978-0-9629142-9-4

First Edition

Printed in the United States by Morris Publishing
3212 East Highway 30
Kearney, NE 68847
1-800-650-7888

Janze Publications
930 Bargo Street
London, KY 40741

Dedicated to

My grandchildren:

Sabin Alexander Anderson Ybarra
Jacob Anthony Anderson Ybarra
Ana Luisa Anderson Ybarra
Coleman Fredy Anderson
Gloria Abelina Anderson

Tomorrow's writers and poets

Thank you to my spouse, family, and friends for their love and support. A special thank you is given to my aunt, Jeune Carpenter Baker, for editing assistance and encouragement in writing.

About the Author

 Pearl Anderson is a Registered Nurse living in Kentucky. She holds a Masters in Social Work with concentration in Gerontology. Her professional career has been in nursing, teaching, health program development and working with the elderly population. She continues to serve as a volunteer nurse with Medical Missions teams to Bryansk, Russia. These experiences have provided much material for story writing and poetry.

Her poetry has appeared in *Poetry as Prayer: Appalachian Women Speak, Kentucky Kaleidoscope,* and five books published by *poetry.com*. She is the mother of three married children and the grandmother of five.

The front cover of *Journey with the Wind* is an acrylic on canvas painting, *Between Seasons,* and the back cover is a pencil and ink drawing, *Lilies*. The art and the handwritten poem are by the author.

Introduction

Journey with the wind

Thoughts on wing;

Through the Countryside—

Gently sing

Come walk with me through the meadows; along the waters'
edge and down the roads of yesteryear; listen to the laughter of
children; sense the smells of the lilacs; see nature all abloom and
taste a bit of God's creation. I pray that there may be one word
or one thought that would help someone along his/her pathway.

Evelyn Pearl

Table of Contents

Journey with the Wind

Table of Contents (continued)

Journey with the Wind

Table of Contents (continued)

Journey with the Wind

i.   *Journey with the wind*

...through the meadows,

Come - Walk

Come walk through the meadow—
Where the grass has grown high and tickles the legs
moving with each step tak'n – no chiggers I beg

Come walk through the meadow—
Smell the honeysuckle's sweetness; pert daisy
swaying in the breeze with Queen Ann's all-lacey

Come walk through the meadow—
Float with the yellow butterfly; Rise up – down
count each precious moment with flowers around

Come walk through the meadow—
Listen to the sounds of cows in yonder field
watch the baby calves romp with such fun they yield

Come walk through the meadow—
Follow narrow path made by others before
dreaming days' dreams while going about their chores

Come walk through the meadow—
Hearken to the birds' lyrical happy songs
resting they sing; while we sense we, too, belong

Come walk through the meadow—
Enjoy the journey with the wind as it blows
gentle breeze against your face; relaxing so

Come walk through the meadow—
Heartily sing louder than the thunder roar
laugh with water's movement, feel the spirit soar

Come walk through the meadow—
See, smell, hear, taste and feel – sweet meditation
experiencing a part of God's creation.

A Morning Prayer

Oh Lord, this is your day
You have allowed me
To open my eyes and see
As you share your beauty
In so many special ways

Oh Lord, I thank you for sharing
E'en when the heart is teary
And the spirit is weary
And the intellect is leery
You bring sunshine in your caring

And now, Lord, I close my eyes
E'en in darkness I see a glow
Soft yellow sunlight shows
Your presence I know
Ev'ry morning is your surprise.

The Leaves and the Wind

Leaves out there quivering on tree
You are moving so free
Unseen wind is blowing your way
The two of you dance – sway

Hanging on the branch as you move
Rhythm of my soul soothes
Watching the movement that is spun
Feel the breeze with your fun.

This Sabbath Morn

Morning peers over the horizon
The miracle of dawning the new day,
Hidden sun reflects light unto clouds
Gladdening our earth with such array

There's a pencil-slim line of golden coral
Where sky and earth seemingly meet,
Pale azure heavens glow in freshness
Slender naked branches reach up to greet

Dear Lord, thank you for mornings color
Gloriously beheld by my eyes,
The purples, aquamarines, rose-orange—
Hues to soften my heart at sunrise.

Morning Sunrise

Arising over yonder hill
Exquisite display thrills
In the dawning of a new day
Brilliant light to survey

Colors beyond comprehension
Present for moment's glance
Golden bar o'er earth's horizon
Glowing into redden

Clouds silently moving away
Into fullness of day
Trees lifting bare limbs in praise
Glorious gift this day.

The Garden

'Twas in the stillness of morning
My thoughts turned to you, Oh Lord
How in your love you made gardens
To refresh – my spirits soared

The green grass glistened with moisture
As sun kissed the dew
A gentle breeze heard in the leaves
With the rustling of you

Listening closely – I heard the birds
Sending messages from work
Amid sweet aromas they sang
Seemingly, not a shirk

Hummingbird fascination held
As your tiny creation
Hums – darts; back and forth; for nectar
Ah! Sweet meditation

Thank you, Lord, for planting gardens
A place for sweet retreat
Here we can pause in nothingness
To find everything; peace.

Flower Garden

Worked in my flower garden today
Crawled pulling weeds away
Pine needles on ground since winter
Picked up with my fingers

Ideas in this spot I bestow
Flowers not in neat rows
Instead, artistically placed
Each within its own space

Coral bells rising from leafy bed
Irises in purple heads
Lilies with long yellow stems
Soon to bloom – yellow gems

Tending a garden there is toil
Fertilizing the soil
Planting and weeding growth abounds
One day – beauty surrounds

Summer Flowers Remain

Chrysanthemums in October
Blooming in early fall
Pretty yellows, mauves and rust-red
Feathery faces small

Impatiens along garden's row
Orange, purple, red and white
Silently greeting all who pass
Four-rounded petals bright

Ah! The summer rose beckons there
A glance not sufficing
Thorns on stems protects the sweetness
Of soft petals enticing

'Tis autumn with tree leaves falling
Warming sun – pouring rain
Garden beauty blooms 'til cold comes
Summer flowers remain

To the Tree Stump

Once upon a time the tree stood
Proudly providing shade around,
Her leaves quivering in the sun
Afternoon refreshment was found,
'Twas weather-beaten through the years
When axed two feet from the ground,
That old tree never really died
As greenish moss to wood is bound,
Now a stump of sculptured beauty –
Once again – green on top around.

Farm Matinee

I looked out on a field today
'Twas one giant bouquet,
Yellow daisy's dancing with ease
Queen Ann's Lace moves in breeze

Carpet of various greens laced
Peplums hanging at waist,
Gently they did sway – to and fro
God's stage on earth – the show

Autumn Tapestries

Far away to high up in sky
Acres of chenille-like puffs rest,
Like a rumpled-old quilt lying
On lumpy feather-bed mattress

Reminds of life's ups and downs
Where dark valley's remain untold –
Climb on up to the mountaintop
Where color begins to unfold

The contrasting of highs and lows
Green pines – red maples seen by all,
Matching the thread pulling one's dreams
Through quilted comforts found in fall

Such is the fabric of life
Seasons come and go in glory,
Happiness blended with strife
Hills and quilts tell their story

The colorful realities lie
Somewhere between the peaks ahead;
Neither, life nor the hills will smooth
As that quilt lying on the bed.

Dancing Leaves

Leaves out there quivering on tree
You are moving so free
Unseen wind is blowing your way
The two of you dance – sway

Hanging on to branch as you move
Rhythm of my soul soothes
Watching the movement that is spun
Feel the breeze with your fun.

Country Sculpture

With coordinated feathers
And colors in the rocks
Brown and white with rusty tail tips
Little bird firmly blocks

So stoic; so calm; no movement
Save the up-down of beak
People round and about do pass
Stop to look – do not speak

Something near reverence exists
So committed alone
Black-ringed neck Killdeer looking ill
Feigning to protect own

Brave they are – nesting on bare ground
Shallow grassed depression
Shrill "kill-dees" by noisy plovers
Protects from transgression

In the country cemetery
Few people come and go
Country sculpture guarding her eggs
Safe by rock seemed to know

God in His greatness showed such love
In creating such as these
Lessons to learn from Killdeer there
Patient protective ease

Little Boys

The park an open field, little boys
Wide-eyed anticipation – much joy,
Mysteries of the grass and dirt awaits
Unable to control selves at gate

Imagination vividly before
Running, laughing, falling some more,
A big bug is seen crawling yonder
Lingering, small lads watch in wonder

Adults find it hard to understand
As they yell to issue a command,
"Stop," "Don't go," "Do as I say – sit down;"
Sitting – until awaited friend found

Up they jump – running "far far" away –
To the next tree where it's safe to play,
Another world comes to little minds
As each new treasure they do find

Occasional preoccupation
In quiet, secret, contemplation
Thinking about last night's video
And, how to become like the hero

Trees to climb; holes to dig; explore
Future scientists on earth's floor,
Mixing soils and bugs with nearby sand
Oh! Me! Little boys, look at your hands!

To the water faucet – a new game
Clean but smelly; more fun just the same,
The present so precious – fleeting fast
Tomorrow's opportunities vast

Today – run after the butterfly
Find the make-believe rabbit in sky,
Climb, climb higher; run faster than wind,
God bless and keep you, my little friends.

Secrets of Nature

Tree standing there covered with snow
Tell how is it you know
Your rough arms so firm and strong
Birds know where they belong

You hold secrets of birds at light
Giving them peace from flight
Talking of their travels and rest
In the spring will build nest

The wind dares not to share what heard
When whistling past the birds
Tree - bird - wind; all safely secure
Secrets in snow assured.

Rain-ing

Rainy day brings
> Time for thoughts
> Sadness is wrought
> Lessons are taught

Rainy day things
> Music in drops
> Sounds on housetops
> Rhythm ne'er stops

Rainy day brings
> Water to drink
> Calm time to think
> Flowers in pink

Rainy day rings
> Circles in spots
> Curly hair in knots
> Laughter a lot

Rainy day brings
> Moisture to soil
> Relief for toils
> Smell of coal oil

Rainy day sings
> Water on wings
> Sounds of harp strings
> God's rich blessings

Unseen

There is beauty in unseen things
   The wind
      And God's love –
Bringing refreshment to the soul
   Physical
      And spiritual
Come – journey to the highest hill
   Breathe in His goodness
Feel the cool breeze of assurance.

ii.   *Journey with the wind*

...along the water's edge,

Reflecting Attitudes

Reflections cast on pond of life
There shines either hope or strife,
Depending on the wind that blows
Attitudes reflect what life shows.

Day Break

Look! Here comes the sun
Over the mountain
The creek below runs
As rippling fountain

I ponder; I muse
Nature's harmony
Gentle sun's movement
Water rush softly

Within my eyes' view
Evidence of God
A mountain protection
Light and water reflection

Thank you, Lord, I say
For giving me this day
Strength gained from nature
Meditation pure

Creekside

I watch the movement of the stream
E're flowing with boundaries
It reminds me of life's dreams
In its solidarity

Always running except in drought—
Giant splash at rock's edge;
Then, gentle trickling in patterns
Peaceful; Oh! Such peaceful hedge

The rains come leaving a large surge
Powerfully with speed
The torrents come with rushing force
With caution one must take heed

All day the waters surely roll
As dreams deep within my soul.

Weep No More

Weeping willow tree by creek's edge
I passed by you this Spring morning
As you stood in graceful display
Your hanging branches were mourning

Weeping willow tree, why so sad?
As your delicate green leaves sway,
Moving so slowly with the wind
Blowing gently on the March day

Fine protection you do offer
Beneath your fresh new greenery
Sorrow overshadowed by strength
You are the most beautiful tree

Supported by your solid trunk—
No more weeping my willow tree
Giving comfort through your sadness
'Tis truly what you mean to me

Weeping Willow Tree

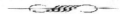

The Stream

Today, I walked by the stream
The water talked – it seemed
The words did flow –
Where will they go?

Nourishing along the way
Flourishing each day
The movement continuous
Motion of water tremendous

Hear the sound – feel the coolness
Calm refreshment blesses
Flowing – meandering, it seems
Into the larger stream

Walking along the path by stream
Creating thoughts – dreaming dreams
Ripples dancing on sunlit water
Small brook leading to when – where

Pattern only seen from above
Charted by Creator's love

The Sun and The Sea

Sunlight glistening on ocean
Sea vast deep and rapid
Lapping waves folding inward
Ruffles pleated amid

Waters' radiant reflections
Transcending earth's limits—
Meditation offered to God
Praise as beauty emits

White foam contrasts dark shadows
As suds in blue basin—
Sea going out bids sweet farewell
'Til tide returns again

Sea Garden Reverie

"Hello," she said to the ocean
Seen so clearly these days
As she watches the birds turned gulls
Soaring over the waves

Feeling the mist ease her pain – she's
Longing for one at sea
As oceans' tide does flow in – out
Oh! The sweet reverie

Country maiden amidst beauty
Thoughts return homeward – sigh!
Where lovely summer flowers grow
In her garden – nearby

Patterns in the Sand

Tides roll in – many gentle waves
Wondrous on which to gaze
Tides go out – past prints erased
Now undulating sands displayed

A new sand canvas twice each day
For sea to sculpt at the most
Our prints lasting hours at the most
For the sea – never still

Moments

Sitting by the wharf on fall day
Birds came – then flew away
Warm breeze – endless summer futile
Quiet moments tranquil

Dry Hill

In the mountains of Kentucky
Where the river runs free
Up on a hill by the Parkway
'Tis morning on Sunday

The Dry Hill Church quietly waits
All who enter her gates,
Stone entryway with bell above
Ready to share Christ's love

Many steps to climb to front door
One, two, three and then, more
With river to back and road between
Climbing higher – grass green

Enter for love, worship and praise
Christ's love to share this day
Community gathered does meet
The fellowship – Oh! So sweet

Little church reflecting God's love
Looking down from above
Witnessing to those passing by
Of faith in Him on high

Beach Stroll

Elder

Beach silhouette

Slow in step – stick in hand

Heightened respect for his attempts

Age'd man

iii.   *Journey with the wind*

...down the roads of yesteryear,

Sulphur Well

Once upon a time in Cloverdale,
Of north Metcalfe County
Ezekiel Neal struck a well
Sulphur was his bounty

'Twas there in eighteen forty-five
Name was changed – fame at hand
Cloverdale became Sulphur Well
Resort built; hope began

A century and half later
Things changed; weathered boards vast
August Sulphur Well Homecoming
People come; talk of past

Music heard across the river
As was played long ago,
Families gathers; small ones playing
Hot afternoon moves slow

Children laughingly throw their rocks
Splashing the water
As they make memories; build dreams—
Wavelike movements still there

Even though the resort is history
The thought of what was stays
Sulphur still smells in the river
Reminder of past days

When Old Friends Meet
(At a Cemetery)

Walking among graves of loved ones
Memories flood the mind;
The one who ran the country store
Was fun and very kind

Next to Grandpa is dear Grandma
Many years have come and gone
Just to think of them love is felt;
Thoughtfully moving on

Looking over toward the truck
Old friend Ruby sits there,
Opal with cane walks to visit
Two friends meet – talk with care

Conversation steady and sweet
Octogenarians
Poor health in fast passing years, yet –
Now, time stands still for friends

Paths of Sam's Childhood

'Twas June fifteenth of '03
Toward home the journey,
Left Georgia – headed for Knoxville,
We traveled through the hills

Conners and Andersons old friends
Stopped for lunch after ten,
Sam made plans to share past in depth
Places of his childhood steps

Up the street to parent's old house
Then home of brother's spouse,
Each stop Sam left car; cane in hand
Walked – shared story with friend

Oral history of early years—
Eighty-plus – disappeared,
Such a treasure to hear from him
Telling stories; such gems

On to Glenwood Cemetery,
"This is where we will be."
Sam's first candy Milky Way here
Granville Conner Road near

Forty-two acres of ground lay
"Moved here when six," he said.
A.B. Bell lived across highway
Where Sam, then, went to play

"Went to the swimming hole," Sam mused
"We never knew which shoes
We were wearing when we came out
Of there," Sam laughed aloud

"Dad had a mattock made to dig
Sassafras bushes bit,
A smaller mattock made for me
To help dig as could be."

At the rear of this farm with spouse
Sam borrowed for first house—
One-thousand five hundred dollars;
Here he accepted callers.

Barn in nineteen twenty-five built
Standing in spot with tilt,
They had cattle and kept some hay
Orchards along the way

On to the next farm; "house still here";
Moved at one and half years.
Judson Conner, his kin
Had an "air-cooled Franklin"

A 'twenty-three car story told
About T-Model Ford,
"Relative left and car did set,"
Sam remembers it yet

Sam belonged to church 'cross road,
To Powell Baptist, Sam strode,
Father was the Choir Director,
"Learned more about God there."

On to Powell Station we did seek
Located by Beaver Creek
Where "dirt to make bricks" was gotten
These times are not forgotten

"Two mules, Beck and Kate," were used here
"With mower and some fear."
The roads with gravel – a modern trek
To Powell Station each week

Groner's General Merchandise
And Post Office enticed,
Cooper's Grocery near on street
Where families did meet

Charged by the month were groceries –
And paid regularly.
Sam shared his yesteryear story
Back in days of glory

There sat Jeanette in car
Patiently sitting there;
Sam reliving his childhood dear—
Walks to school for twelve years

Story as told; written in rhyme
Memories of old time
The years have passed on; none so sweet—
The paths walked with child's feet.

(Note: Sam passed away a few months later.)
EPA

Friendship

To be friends for so very long
'Tis valuable real estate
Carefully preserved without knowing
Endless time fails to separate

Like a vapor o'er earth's rich soil
Friendship lingers, leaves or returns
Sometimes more dense that 'twas before
Then, at times, for which the heart yearns

The binding that should not unravel
With soft threads woven and secured
Left alone can fade and weaken
Yet, when found, through time has endured

Ah! Through life, one must till and weave
To carefully preserve the past,
One day; some day; someone; may come
Recalling, rekindling so vast.

There's something magical that comes
As shared memories are opened
One's importance validated—
Remembering those things again

Knowing one cares is very sweet
With tilling and weaving we've wept
Friendship found more valuable
Than all earthly possessions kept

A Farmer's Morning

In the morning of summer day
Dew on the green grass lay
Farmer's chores must be done
His full day has begun

He goes to the barn through the gate
Rushing not to be late
Horses out beyond the fences
Need to plow the trenches

Rumbling heard in the western sky
There's work to do – Oh! My!
Just when the horses come around
The rain came pouring down

Back in the barn he's soaking wet
Too much to do to fret
Hanging the harness, cleaning stalls,
Day dreaming as rain falls

Blackberry Picking on the Fleming County, Kentucky Farm

"Come on we're picking blackberries,"
Dad would call out and say,
Brother and I would get pans and
Dad a bucket for the day

Out the back door and through the gate
Past the barn through the grass,
The three of us off to the back field
On our way to the patch

Mom was at the house a-waiting
Each wonderful berry
For blackberry cobbler to make,
Sister would be merry!

Back in the field were ripe berries
We picked and picked them well,
Our hands, face and mouth were purplish
From dripping juice that fell

The June bug was e'er present
With his soft buzzing sound,
His presence remained on the berry
Known by the taste we found

Berries were canned in tummies
We picked and ate with glee,
The extra went into the pails by
My Dad, brother and me

There would come a summer shower
Fast – get under the tree,
Dad would laugh and tell a story
The rain o'er – get busy

Soon our buckets would be heaping
With the purple jewels,
As back to the house we went, all
Purple stained and tummy's full

From the kitchen smells of cobbler
Filled the air with delight
We were excited to sample
Our great harvest tonight

Blackberry Picking's Next Day

Oh! Dear! What is all this itching?
Scratch, scratch is all I do
There are bright red whelps all over
Many instead of few

Yesterdays' fun in the berries
Yields to chiggers today
But, the thought of cobbler's taste
Helps take the itch away.

Around and Around

Over in the blackberry patch
June bugs are a-hummin'
Dad and children have been pickin'
Winter, it's a-comin'

Time to go home; jobs done
June bug is caught in flight
For the children to have some fun
Before supper tonight

String on June bug with child on end
Hold on tight; stay on legs,
Around and around fast they go
"My turn," the child begs

Quickly the children become tired
And the June bug is freed—
Shaken unharmed return's home
To the berries with speed

Happy and laughing the children
All falling on the ground,
Told how they and the June bug
Went around and around

The thoughts of work and play have changed
Within memories time,
My mind goes around and 'round in
June bug and berry rhyme.

Saturday Nights

Flemingsburg on Saturday nights
An absolute delight
A rural farm town in Kentucky
In the early fifties

Let's get the work done-up Dad said
Cows were milked chickens fed
Water heated for baths in tub –
A galvanized rub

Hand-made dresses and hair slicked-down
Ready to go to town
The family in Chevy car
"Everyone" would be there

The Princess Theater we'd go
To watch a picture show
A western with Tom, Roy or Gene
"Yippy-ya yay" on screen

Fifty cents was our allowance
For ticket popcorn plus
Change left over for us to spend
At Village Grill with friends

Some went through Mrs. Hall's or
Colgan's Restaurant door
Fans would whirl up on the ceiling
Keeping all cool feeling

They laughed and talked out on the street
Dad and his friends would meet
Boys cruised whistled under the moon
Girls would giggle and swoon

Cut Rate, Mr. Doyle or Bob Klee's
Where one bought groceries
Women discussed their home and dreams
The price of eggs and creams

There were other stores for shopping
Fischer's for a new ring,
Lerman's or Fried's for clothes galore
Hinton's five and ten store

Spencer and Leslie's had TV
We viewed what was to be,
Wright's Hardware by the railroad track
Tools were found on the rack

Emmon's or Aikin's the drug stores
Had helps for aches or more
The Bon Ton with country ham treat
Bus stop across the street

For some men – McGregor's pool hall
Their chili best of all
Nearby was Browning and McKee's
Furniture a-plenty

Rankin's Hatchery outside town
Feed and feed sacks were found
Saturday nights were a ball
Flemingsburg had it all

The corners of Water and Main
All four buildings the same
Diagonally faced around
One column roof to ground

Old Court House stood on the hill crown
Overlooked active downtown
With Fleming Creek flowing through
There before town was new

Candy cigarettes were such fun
Friends and neighbors were one,
Every single Saturday
Family time to play

Groceries and items to suit
Were placed in the car boot
Drove home – family together
In all types of weather

Fleming County Court House, Flemingsburg, Kentucky -- License Tag 1950
(Picture – Courtesy of Fleming County Public Library)

By Gate of Childhood

Around the curve and up the road
Over to left – turn there
Gate to front field and childhood home
By post and cornflower

Straight ahead up the hill to next
Big old farmhouse did stand
Weathered old gray barn up on right
Where tobacco stripped by hand

A creek ran gently under road
Near where the mailbox leaned
Cards and letters from family
Happy thoughts were sent it seemed

The creek, mailbox and cornflower
Beautiful rural scene
Children waiting for the school bus
Morning sunlight did beam

Fresh milk for market was picked up
Loaded on truck with smile
Taken to Maysville for the sale
Money returned in while

Friends – neighbors would wave in passing
All things had a reason
The rains came and the creek would flood
Time moved along in seasons

The farm though now gone as was known
Holds warmth so very dear
The old metal gate open'd – closed
Throughout all the years

The Old Homestead

Once a beautiful new farmhouse
Built on earth's meadow land,
A sweet home for a family
Crafted by loving hand.

Husband and wife together worked
Growing food, planting flowers
Tilling the soil, clearing land and –
Resting at evening's hour.

The children within came and went
Spring's daffodils bloomed o'er.
Summers' green turned to autumns' red,
Leaves falling on porch floor

Generations have gone away
Leaving memories vast
Yellow daffodils remember –
Blooming same as in past.

Gray boards held by yesteryear's nails
Have weathered rain and snow,
Now stand as a testimony
Of a day long ago

The house which once sheltered many,
Has roof of rusting tin.
Now, homestead belongs to nature,
As wind and rain move in.

Ah! Old house surveying your landscape,
What is it you could say?
Tell tales of births, struggles and deaths
To help us live each day

(Note: First published in *Kentucky Kaleidoscope*, 2006, by the
London Writer's Group. *EPA*)

Farm Life Changed

Electricity came to farm
In nineteen forty-five,
New life began with lights at nights
Stay up late – lands alive!

No more washing on the wash board
No stove heating the iron
Gone is old kitchen cooking stove
New way of baking born

Music and stories came from box
Turn the dial – plug in wall,
Radio connected to world
There on farm – heard it all

Refrigeration kept food cold
Moms' ice tea always there,
Ice for the work hands' cold water
New treats for all to share

Life was good with pleasures abound
More light, more work, less rest;
Farm workers worked longer – harder,
Wonder which days were best?

To the Mailbox

Ode to the metal container
Communication center,
Family name across the side
Proudly tells who abides

Rounded top on old wooden post
Simplicity does boast,
Standing quietly day in – day out
Remains steady no doubt

Blue cornflowers growing around
Goldenrod can be found,
The creek flowed with water rippling
Nearby the birds do sing

The country mailbox has a charm
Beautifies the farm,
Standing proudly straight and strong
At end of driveway long

Protects in weather of kinds;
Rain hail sleet snow sunshine.
Mail kept clean dry safe from damage
Letters with kind words from sage

Flag to raise and door to open
Check coming – we're hopin'
Red flag up signals mail to send
Read flag down – reading begins

A sweet note from Auntie dear
She sent message of cheer,
A postcard from far away friend
Telling of health on mend

Girl's heart races – letter from beau
The newspaper enjoyed so,
Oh! Mailbox, we place trust in you
To share all that is new

Pranksters stole box at Halloween
Such fun they did glean,
Dad out next morning; up-down lanes
Mailbox found – home again

The mailman – careful and timely
Delivers faithfully,
Red dress from catalog he brings
And baby chicks in Spring

We pray that God will protect all
So important a call,
The mailman, mailbox and letters
In concert – life better.

After the Rain

The afternoon rain had fallen
Pouring down on the farm
'Tis too wet to hoe crops in field
Creeks swollen – no alarm

Walking to-from fields by highway
Farmer wears his high boots
There he moves the scythe with sickle long
Cutting grassy upshoots

Sickle blade 'tis silvery and sharp
Swishing fast through the air
Whisk! Whisk! The tall green grass does fall
Scythe moved back-forth with flair

His muscular arms thick and taunt
Move rhythmic in wet
His broad hand holding handle firm
As task before was set

Seemingly, grass high as farm's debt
Both attacked – left and right
Happiness found in cleaner fields –
Time for chores before night

Soon the crickets are heard – grass cut
Now to finish work day
Sickle dried, placed in shed; cows milked,
Farmer has special ways

Close of day has come upon earth
Headed for home and meal
Satisfaction mixed with fatigue—
Having served God with zeal

Echo

From house through valley – an echo
      "HELLO...
            Hello...
                Hello..."
Heard repetitively o'er and o'er
As on and on it roared

Children out playin laugh with glee
Hearing voice cannot see
Each takes turn to see whom loudest
That one is the proudest

The say "listen" with all aglow
      "HELLO...
            Hello...
                Hello..."
And "hear my voice come back to me"
Such fun and all for free.

Alikeness

Clouds were layered in sky today
Floating gathering billows
Sunshiny white and watery gray
Many fluffy pillows

Piled high against the couch of blue
With irregular shapes and design
Blending color milieu
All balanced – suspended so fine

Brightest white celestially
Darkest gray nearest ground
'Twas extraordinarily
Akin to life around

iv.   *Journey with the wind*

...through glimpses of long ago,

Comfort

As summer's days come to an end,
the outside temperatures fall,
thoughts turn toward home and comfort
and the one thing cherished by all.
The Complicated Nine Patch quilt
stitched by Ma many years ago,
with a few patches of fabric—
needle and thread by hand, she sewed.

October has come once again,
four decades since she passed away,
still the Complicated Nine Patch
stirs untold stories to this day.
My imagination runs high
seeing Rachel's blue calico,
a bit of Gertrude's red plaid dress
all pinned in place for hand to sew

There's leftover fabric found
from Frances's bright yellow blouse,
and the green floral that Jeune wore
to the party at the school house.
I suspect that Ma found more scraps
tucked deep down in a sewing box,
pulled out with loving memories
as pattern cut—thoughts unlocked.

Through the years, her sons took brides,
Nola Mae and Toolee they wed,
quilting became a family art,
making warm covers for their beds.
Triangles and squares clipped with care,
pinned and basted 'til design complete,
ten stitches per inch was good work
each section was then pressed so neat.

Repetitive designs complete,
then blocks added in contrast,
when the desired size was reached.

Filling and backing added last.
Now the quilting began—each stitch
meticulously, one by one,
within frames where quilt firmly held
to ensure no puckers before done.

O'er half-a-century has past
yet each tiny stitch still in place,
three generations' memories
woven together and embraced.
Ma's Complicated Nine Patch—
treasure made many years before,
bound with hopes and dreams pulled by thread,
shared at summer's ending once more.

Windmills in Holland

It was in my first grade class (1945-46) at Flemingsburg Elementary School, Flemingsburg, Kentucky that I saw my first windmill. Mrs. Cray Borders (women used the husband's name back then) was our teacher. I doubt she ever realized what a master she was at creating memories in the minds of the young children. I don't know if any of my classmates have similar memories but she created a fascinating world for me.

I remember seeing this windmill in the spring of 1946. Because we were coloring pictures of tulips, I'm sure it had to have been in the springtime because of the seasonal association. Tulips were not the only pictures we colored. We colored pictures of wooden shoes; windmills and anything associated with Holland. As we colored, Mrs. Borders read us stories about Holland. I believe we even practiced our writing skills by writing words unique to Holland. After our pictures were colored, they were hung at the top of the blackboard. They were for our admiration and her "travel" plans.

One day, after a couple or three weeks, Mrs. Borders came into the classroom carrying manila folders. She told us that we were going on a trip. You talk about excitement! Most of the class, like me, was from a farming family. A trip, to us, was going to town (Flemingsburg) on a Saturday night or school on Monday. A "real trip" would be going to Maysville when the tobacco sold. This was a long eighteen miles away on cold and icy winter mornings.

On each folder, Mrs. Borders had placed our "passport." On wide lined yellow writing paper, our "passports" were meticulously cut (about 3" X 4") and clipped to the outside of the manila folder. She had very carefully printed our names, our birth date, and stapled a small picture of each of us on our individual "passports." As there were, probably, at least 30 children in that classroom, one can only imagine the time that must have taken! Mrs. Borders had placed all of our individual pictures and papers we had written related to our "Holland " study inside our manila folder – our "attaché case."

She gave each of us our passport, clipped to our "case" as we were placed in line. She told us to be very quiet. We were going to get on a "boat" that day and go to Holland. We were so excited! We had to keep the excitement quiet and did just what she asked of us. She was our teacher, we respected her, and she was taking us on a trip.

In the Flemingsburg Elementary School (where the Fleming County Library now stands) the wooden floors had a sharp smell of being freshly oiled, as found in many old school floors. On this floor, twenty or thirty 6-year-olds quietly lined up in the hallway on their way to Holland. The floor of the auditorium was slanted slightly down toward the stage. This gave the illusion that we were walking up the gang-plank to a boat. Climbing onto the "boat," Mrs. Borders told us to be very careful. We remained in the dark area just off the stage. The stage curtain was closed. There was a very small window on the exterior wall across the stage, off to our left. As we were all facing the door we had just entered, Mrs. Borders proceeded to tell us yet another story about Holland.

In a few minutes, she said, "we are here." Looking around, I saw the most beautiful windmill out that window. It was far more wonderful than ever imagined. That is all I remember – that one incredible windmill. I don't even recall getting off the boat.

About forty years later, my husband and I had an opportunity to go to Europe. Our three children, then in college, agreed – and assured that Mom could go to Holland to see a real windmill. (They had been told the above story so many times during their early years.)

We went to the Netherlands, or Holland, and, yes, I saw a windmill. It looked exactly like the one I had seen out of that "boat window" inside the elementary school auditorium. In fact,

in my mind's eye, the windmill in the window from 1946 was far more vivid than the real one I stood by in 1985.

The Soft and Gentle Art of Teaching

Mrs. Olivia Pryor was a widow lady who lived with her daughter. She had come from Alabama originally. She and her husband had pastored a Presbyterian Church just prior to his death. She was just like her name sounded – soft and gentle.

Her white hair was worn back in a round bun. She just looked the part of a warm and loving schoolteacher.

It was in 1947-48 in Fleming County, Kentucky that I entered the third grade. I loved Mrs. Pryor from the beginning because she asked me to hold the flag on the first day of school. I felt so important standing there in front of my class. My friend, Juanita, told me years later that her feelings weren't quite the same as mine because she was unable to hold the flag on the first day of school. It must be tough on a teacher having to live with the results of those "first day of school" remembrances.

Our classroom was the only room in the school that had a pot bellied stove which burned wood to heat the room. We were in the basement of the building by the side of the furnace room. There were no heat ducts or registers placed into this room. The ducts all went to the upstairs. Somehow placing wood in the stove did not seem fitting for a nice person like Mrs. Pryor. She never complained. I believe the janitor helped to keep the fire going.

My friends were Mary, Mittie and Juanita. We tried real hard to be the best in the class. Back then, the teachers would announce who did the best. This method of teaching worked for me but I am not sure it did for the others.

I missed some school that year, but not as much as the previous year. I had a milder form of Scarlet Fever that was known as Scarletina. My home was not quarantined during this illness as it had been the previous year. I recall Mary writing me a letter and sending it with my homework that her mother brought over to our farmhouse. I must have spent much time in reading and writing as I gained the strength to return to my favorite place – school.

I recall returning to school following our Christmas break. As I was writing letters of the alphabet on the blackboard, someone asked me what I did during Christmas. I distinctly remember saying, "Oh, I practiced my script writing." This has always been an interesting recollection for me, as I don't recall being particularly interested in handwriting.

One day when Mrs. Pryor was ill and had to be absent from school, we had a substitute teacher. The substitute's first day with us was not good. Mrs. Pryor had a beautiful large sheet of heavy glass over her desk and the, ever-present, paddle was to the side. Under this glass, Mrs. Pryor would place her items of importance. She kept this glass very clean. The students were proud of the glass top because Mrs. Pryor had the nicest desk of all our teachers. The substitute teacher had a big temper and was very nervous. The class was not responding in the way she, apparently, thought appropriate. She reached over, picked up the paddle and brought it down hard on the desk. Wham! Crack! She broke Mrs. Pryor's beautiful glass desktop along with our hearts in seeing the glass broken. We were so stunned the rest of the day that I doubt we learned much from the books.

Mrs. Pryor returned to school. We were all waiting in anticipation of what she would say or do about her desk's broken glass. She remained soft and gentle; never saying a word about the incident or asking any questions. This was a valuable lesson for us. We may have learned more in her absence and return than if she had been present and teaching.

Caught and Swung by "The Best"
(Or "The Flying Boys")

Miss Bess just might have had some explaining to do! The bold way in which she reprimanded some of the boys in the classroom would, most probably, levy some heavy charges now, but her discipline method was certainly effective back then. Miss Bess was the sixth grade teacher at the Flemingsburg Elementary School back in 1950-51.

Miss Bess, a short lady, was about one-half as wide as she was tall. At about 50 years of age, she seemed old to me. I think she seemed old because she was my father's teacher at the old Washington School. She would tell me stories about my father, "Orville Jones"; how he would walk slowly through the snow-laden fields and would often be late for school. Miss Bess told me that she would question him as to why He was late. She said that he would always grin and say that he had been "chasing rabbits through the fields."

My father was 29 years older than I so Miss Bess would have been very young when she was his teacher. I would guess about 19 years old. Given those estimates, it is certain that she had had many years of practice in the handling of young schoolboys. Miss Bess dyed her hair a shoe polish black color. When she was out in the sun with the class, she always had her umbrella up so that her hair color wouldn't fade. She wore her hair short, parted in the middle, and had it permanent waved. She kept her hair tidy against her head with a hair net. In those days, teachers never came to the classroom without a nice dress on and color coordinated with pretty, well-polished dress shoes. Her hair and attire only added to the overall professional appearance of this remarkable sixth grade teacher.

There were generally three or four boys who would get in trouble for misbehaving on a regular basis. For the life of me, I cannot remember what they did.

They were just misbehaving. Today, through my mind's eye, I can still see my cousin lofting through the air. Miss Bess would snag an offending boy by the waist of his pants. She would then pick him up and swing him around and around attached only by her hand holding to the back of the boys' belt. My cousin wasn't the only one, but he was the one regularly caught. I do recall watching another little boy being "flown around" through the air as if he were on a carnival ride. His name was Jerald.

That Miss Bess had to have been one strong lady. I think she had been practicing this method of discipline for many years as her biceps were well developed.

The toughest part for the boys came after three to four swings round in circles. She brought them down flat on their feet. She kept her left hand on their belt at their waist, then raised her right hand to shake her finger in their face. Looking them straight in the eye, she would chant, "Be sure your sins will find you out!" This had to have been just awful for the boys. I suspect they were very dizzy.

This is where, I think, the PTA would, now, come down on her – threatening those boys and all. This was the worst form of discipline that I can recall her ever using. Despite the "strong arming" the boys, she did hold the love, respect and attention of her sixth grade class.

The WLW Radio Station out of Cincinnati had a "Best Teacher" contest. I wrote a letter nominating Miss Bess. I think the reason I nominated her was she had taught my father as well as me. That made her extra-special to me. Anyway, she won the contest. She never knew that I had entered her in the contest until she received her award letter.

Miss Bess took me aside to let me know that while she appreciated being thought of, she strongly recommended that none of the other teachers find out. I'm guessing now that she probably did not like whirling those boys around. She just wanted them to be respectable, well-rounded young men who were able to stand on their own two feet.

If We Had the Money

It was recess and ice cream – yum!
Not much money for some
There stood Jim holding the big bucks
Buy us one? No such luck!

Many years later – ice cream thoughts
Those "sticks" we could have bought
Unmelted – remain in our minds
Money – we could not find

Funny how the memories last
Motion pictures of past
Ice cream and money – desired things
That life's recess brings

Eden's Chapel

Introduction

"Eden's Chapel" is a fascinating place. It is located in Fleming County, Kentucky out of Hillsboro on the Sunset Road. The names of Hillsboro, Sunset and Eden's Chapel, alone, conjure up a visual image of beauty. One can see the foothills of the Appalachian Mountains along the eastern horizon.

Eden's Chapel lies between Sunset and the Mouth of the Fox on Licking River.

At one time there was a school and a Methodist Church located at Eden's Chapel. There is a cemetery named the Eden's Chapel Graveyard that lies near where the old church and schoolhouse once stood.

I began thinking about Eden's Chapel after receiving some Internet Rootsweb messages related to the early people of this place located in rural Northeast Kentucky.

In one message dated 19 September 2000, Gordon T. Weaver, Jr. wrote, *"Benjamin Eden is recorded in the 1850 Census. He is mentioned as 'Eaton' in court records of Fleming 1848 in regards to a dispute between David Weaver and others, including Wm. Denton, Richard Vanlandingham and Squire Day. A fellow researcher noted that Eden Cemetery is in fact the same as the Republican Meeting House Cemetery where George Philip Weaver was buried in 1814. The land once belonged to Geo. P. Weaver as contended in the court records."* Mr. Weaver went on to request information related to Weavers buried in Eden Cemetery.

John Vice posted a reply on 18 October 2000 that read, *"The old church building that was the Eden's Chapel Church stood just across the road from the Eden's Chapel Cemetery. For several years, the church building was used as a barn to store hay. The*

building has since collapsed and now is gone. *"But, as of now, the old Eden's Chapel Cemetery continues to be kept mowed & cleaned..."*

On 31 March 2002, Jackie Presley responded, *"My grgr-uncle was Benjamin F. Eden – who donated the land for Eden's Chapel Cemetery. When I visited the cemetery back in 1980's, it was totally overgrown. Now, that it is being maintained I would like to contact those people responsible for doing such a wonderful service and make a contribution to their efforts."*

John Vice on 02 April 2002 sent an E-mail where he listed the genealogical names of his family who lived in *"the Eden's Chapel area are McKee, Galliher (a variation of the spelling for Gallagher), Day, Leforge, Wills, and Hunt."*

In reviewing the list of burials in the "Eden's Chapel Graveyard, Fleming County, Kentucky" compiled by Pat McAlister, copyright 1997, I see that there have been 13 Eden family members buried there, including Benjamin F. Eden (1803-1881). The earliest members of the Eden family buried in the Eden's Chapel Graveyard were Jeremiah (1772-1859) and his wife, Mary (1769-1850). The last burial for an Eden family member was in 1908. She was Jane Eden (1819-1908) the wife of Andrew (1811-1888).

John Vice's great-great grandparents, John S. Galliher (1836) and his wife, Ellen McKee (1836-1914) and great-great-great grandparents, William (1801-1889) and Abigail Boyd McKee (1805-1885) are listed as being buried at the Eden's Chapel Graveyard. There were no family names listed other than "Day." Neither Andrew Trumbo Day nor his wife, Martha Jane Leforge Day are listed.

A listing for a Weaver family member has not been found in either, the Eden's Chapel Graveyard or the nearby New Hope Graveyard listings. The Old Republican Meeting was apparently held at Eden's Chapel; however, there seems to be a separate graveyard somewhere near Eden's Chapel.

John Vice had written in his E-mail: *"I have never ran into any information at all about Eden's Chapel. Several old school pictures are published from time to time in the Flemingsburg newspapers, but I have never seen one for Eden's Chapel."*

The Church

On April 03, 2002, I called Katherine (Kirk) Riley, a first cousin of my mother, Nola Mae (Conway) Carpenter, to gather some historical information. Katherine's mother, Effie, was a sister to Isaac Leslie Conway the father of my mother. Katherine was born on December 10, 1911. She has a marvelous mind and is so willing to share her recollections. This seemed to be the perfect time to try to capture a few memories related to Eden's Chapel.

Katherine recalled that she was seven years old when she and her brother, Glenn, moved to Eden's Chapel with their parents, Claude and Effie (Conway) Kirk. She said that they began attending church at the Eden's Chapel Methodist Church.

Katherine said that she remembers three of the pastors. They were "Brother Armitage, Brother Wells and a Brother Tanner." They would be assigned by the Kentucky Methodist Conference for about a two-year assignment. The church service was held on Sunday afternoons alternating the time of service every other Sunday. "One Sunday, Sunday School would be at 1:00 PM with church at 2:00 PM. The next Sunday it would be reversed with church at 1:00 PM and Sunday School at 2:00 PM" stated Katherine. The Prayer Meeting was held on Thursday evenings.

Katherine said that there was an organ in the church house and that Ola Story would play the organ. On the Sundays, that Mrs. Story was unable to be there, another lady would play. "She could not play the organ very well but she tried" Katherine recalled.

Ola Story (1903-1996) married Arl Colliver in 1945 and moved to Ohio. Ola was the daughter of Marion and Sallie M. Turner Story. Ola and Arl are buried in the Hillsboro Cemetery.

When Katherine was about 12 or 13 years old, the church sold the organ and purchased a piano. Lola Rawlings was the church pianist with Flora Allene (Story) Conway assisting as needed. Flora Allene was a cousin to the former organist, Ola Story. Flora Allene Story (1913-1986) married William Raymond Conway. Flora was the daughter of Allen Dearing and Hannah Lytle Story. Flora and Wm. Raymond are buried in the Fleming County Cemetery, Flemingsburg, Kentucky.

I mentioned to Katherine about my great-uncle, Jesse Emmons, telling me about how he could not wait until church services were over so that he could get to the back of the church building where Maude Conway was. He said that as soon as the prayer was over, he would take those long legs of his and leap over the pews to her. He was afraid someone else would beat him. Katherine said that had to have been at Eden's Chapel because that "was the only place we went."

Flora A. Story Conway kept a detailed diary during the early 1930's. Her daughter, Linda Conway Owen, graciously shared the diary with permission for me to excerpt written notes pertaining to Eden's Chapel. I am doing so in order to give the reader a feel for Eden's Chapel in the 1930's and its importance to the small rural community. Eden's Chapel is referred to as the "Chapel" in Flora's notes.

November 7, 1930 – *Went to Prayer Meeting and to Pie Supper and Chapel. Wilson and Plummer (Rawlings) came down to school house with Goldie and I. Plummer was with Goldie and Marvin and Red (Raymond Conway) put me up on the Beauty Contest. We went out there with Lola and Gene.*

April 5, 1931 – *Went to Chapel wore my coat. Owsley preached Goldie, Elaine, Geneva, Bertha and Wilson all there also Lola Gene. Went to church tonite Lola and Gene(Rawlings) went with us. Wilson, Goldie, Geneva and Eldon (Perkins) there, saw Emery (Reeder) once.*

June 18, 1931 – *Lola & Gene (Rawlings) and us went to help clean the church at Eden's Chapel took dinner and had a nice time."*

On February 16, 1936, Nola Mae Conway noted in her diary that she had attended two funerals on that day at "Chapel."

Katherine recalls that at one time there were over 60 people who attended the church services at Eden's Chapel. Then, "it got down to less than 25" in attendance. Katherine said that the services continued for some time with only one person, Ora Turner, in attendance. Finally, the church was closed with the memberships of the congregation moved to the Hillsboro Methodist Church.

In the ensuing years, the church was used as a barn as written by Mr. Vice and cited earlier.

The School

The Eden's Chapel School was located "below the church (towards Hillsboro)," according to Katherine. In later years, Mr. Perkins purchased the school building and moved it directly across the road from the original location. Mr. Perkins used the school as a "hog house."

Katherine recalled the names of the teachers she had while attending this one room, grades 1-8, schoolhouse. Her first teacher was Nannie Davis. Katherine said that she was the "pet" of this teacher.

The second teacher was May Phillips. May rode horseback from Grange City. She would "hook the horse up in the shade" while she went inside to teach. "Every morning each child would stand and say a Bible verse" stated Katherine. May was a first cousin, through the Newmans, to Effie (Conway) Kirk the mother of Katherine.

Eulene (Boyd) Rice was the third teacher and the "best" according to Katherine. The year would have been around 1919.

Katherine's fourth teacher was Robert Phillips, the son of May. Fred McGregor was the fifth teacher that Katherine recalls. Mr. McGregor lived in Plummers Landing so he boarded with Dora Ratliff and taught two years at the school.

John Waltz was Katherine's sixth teacher. He lived on Ringos Road and road horseback, as did some earlier teachers.

The last teacher was Owen B. Storey. Mr. Storey boarded with Nettie and Cook Bettis. Mrs. Bettis would fix a lunch for Mr. Storey. He "liked big dried butter (lima) beans." Nettie would bring his lunch to him.

Katherine mentioned that she had always cooked. She would cook fried potatoes and place in between the biscuit. Sometimes, they would have cake that had been made in a muffin pan. She said they always had something to eat. Occasionally, Effie would fry chicken the night before and "save out the best pieces for Glenn and me to take to school the next day." Katherine further stated that "Glenn liked peanut butter but I never did like it." They would take their lunch in a half gallon bucket with holes punched in the top. These holes allowed air to circulate and keep the "biscuit from getting soggy before we ate them."

When asked what they would have to drink, Katherine responded that there was a long hallway at the front entrance of the school. In that hallway, a table stood where a bucket of water would be placed along with a common dipper. When the bucket was out of water, the teacher would assign two pupils to walk to the well for water and carry the refilled bucket of water back to school. Two different pupils were sent each time that water was needed.

Beth Eula Basford Ramey said "Eden's Chapel was a good school with good teachers." She shared this at the 2002 Conway Family Get-Together at Sunset, Kentucky.

The boy and girl "back houses" were separated. The girls' back house (toilet) was toward "Lucy Porters" with the boys' being toward the church.

I am not sure of the year of the last class at Eden's Chapel but it was probably in 1937, the year that the Hillsboro Consolidated School doors were opened for classes. WPA built the new Hillsboro School.

The social life of the children during this time was work, which would begin as soon as they got home from school. Everyone had his/her chores to do. The only time the children would see each other, when not in school, was at Sunday School and church. Katherine laughed as she told some of the stories and said, "Oh, I have had a time!"

Nola Mae, my mother, was awarded a wooden chalk box, which I have, after winning a school spelling bee at Eden's Chapel.

Katherine was able to identify near every student in an Eden's Chapel School picture belonging to Nola Mae (Conway) Carpenter.

About the Eden's and Other History

Katherine mentioned that the only Eden that she ever knew was "Uncle Lit" Eden. "Uncle Lit" never married and always went by that name. He worked around the neighborhood and "took care of Eden's Chapel Graveyard for years" stated Katherine. Others who knew him called him "Uncle Lit, too."

According to John Vice, "Lit" Eden's real name was David Lidster Eden. He was born in June of 1866. John writes that Joseph, Lit's father; Melvina, Lit's mother; Thomas W., a brother; and Mamie, a sister, are all buried at Eden's Chapel. I only find a listing for Mamie on the Eden's Chapel Burial List. She was born in 1870 and died in 1871 having lived only 9 days. "Lit" had another sister, Sarah (born about 1869) and another brother, Minor E. Eden (born about 1876). Both Sarah and Minor had died before "Lit" passed away in 1932.

Jacob Eden was the paternal grandfather of "Lit." Jacob (1801-1868) is listed as being buried at Eden's Chapel.

"Lit" Eden died in Lexington, Kentucky on May 14, 1932 and was buried in the Hillsboro Cemetery (according to his death certificate). John Vice, wrote via E-mail on April 05, 2002, "*I have never checked, but suspect he doesn't have a marker at his grave. The reason I say this is that he owned a house and lot (I have been shown where it was at) which was located about ½ mile past the Eden's Chapel Cemetery. When he died, he had no descendants and the Fleming County Circuit Court searched out all his closest relatives.*"

Virgil Turner, now deceased, once told John Vice that "Lit" Eden took care of the Eden's Chapel many years by cleaning the graveyard with a grasshook, scythe, and his bare hands. John adds, "unlike what people see with lawnmowers and weed-eaters' today.

My great-grandfather, Dr. William Henry Conway and wife, Martha Ann (Newman) Conway are buried at Eden's Chapel, as well as the maternal ancestors of Martha Ann Newman. Dr. Conway (1854-1923) provided medical care for the people of this section of Fleming County during the late 19th – early 20th centuries.

Martha Ann descended from Thomas and Leah Davis Havens. Stephanie (Johnson) Denton has listed some of the Fleming County surnames descending from Thomas and Leah Havens: Havens, Walton, Rice, Hurst, Newman, Todd, Rawlings, Day, Conway, Kirk, Carpenter, Story, Owens, Crain, Arnold, Saunders, Vice, McRoberts, Foudray.

Perhaps, this recollection of Eden's Chapel school, church and graveyard will stimulate someone's memory and additions can be made to this story. Nola Mae loved Eden's Chapel school and church. Others who were privileged to attend this one-room school and church in Eden's Chapel, Fleming County, Kentucky, share this same sentiment.

Eden's Chapel

Eden's Chapel – a place so dear
In days of yesteryear
Where husbands and wives dreamed their dreams
Guided by God Supreme

Children were taught in one-room school
They learned the Golden Rule
Pie socials and spelling bees
Neighbors met and were free

Families worshipped and they prayed
Hymns were sung – music played
In the church of long long ago
Only a few now know

A graveyard is all that remains
Chiseled stones with dates and names
Tells of those who lived and worked here
       Eden's Chapel – so dear.

Children at Eden's Chapel School around 1920

First Row: L to R Lucian Basford, Nola Mae Conway, Katherine Kirk, Lottie McDonald, ? (head down), Hazel Basford, Ollie Riddle, Clayton Basford, Raymond Conway.

Second Row: Norman Turner, Vearl Turner, Grace Moore, Lula Moore, ?, Robert McDonald (?), Ransom Todd, Lee Copher (hands over face).

Third Row: Arthur Harmon, Leslie "Lal" Harmon, Ester Gray, Dayton Gray, Sterling Porter, Mildred Ratliff, Katherine McDonald, Howard Basford (behind Raymond)

(Identified by Katherine Kirk Riley)

Old Eden's Chapel School, Fleming County, Kentucky

Christmases of Yore

There stood a weather-boarded log house
In the northern part of the southland
Where the hills rolled towards the creekbed
Then, up over the horizon and

There the crops had been sown, grown and plowed –
Following the harvest of the fall,
Hay lifted to barn loft; corn in crib;
Garden food canned; winter's food for all

Burley leaves were stripped with firm "hand" made
Pressed to go to market – best of town,
Soon the auctioneer would bellow out
The price until a buyer was found,

'Twas a joyful day for the farmers
Time to go home – settle for winter
Money in the pocket; at least half –
Rest to the tenant farmers' owner.

The snowflakes start falling from the sky
Be about piled up by gateposts' corner
Blinding snow making it hard to drive
Seems to be coming early this winter

'Tis time to buy coal, kerosene oil
Need to keep the children warm with care;
Plus, Christmas is coming very soon
Tinge of excitement hangs in the air

Daddy would tease about what might come;
There was no long list for lots of stuff –
Expectations not great from Santa;
A little doll would be quite enough.

v.   Journey with the wind

...beyond the horizon,

Totti and Sabin

Sabin age five, Totti age two,
Brothers with much to do
Sat on bench temporarily
What next is there to see?

Totti is only there for while
Finding water his style
Sabin sits seriously in thought
Contemplates – who knows what?

Their every movement brings joy
This from two little boys
Whether throwing small rocks or balls
They are a treat for all.

Third Grader's Departing Gift

Lying in bed
    Listening to the morning sounds—

When...
    Ever so gently the door opened

Entering quietly
    He walked to the bed,
        Him with his black hair

Placing my arms around him—
    "Oh Sabin, I'm going to miss you"
        "Me, too," he said.

He turned around
    Leaving to go to school
        I was left with a precious memory

A Spoonful of Supper

"A spoonful of peaches
Makes the zucchini
    Go
        down— "
Zucchini go down—
A spoonful of peaches
Makes the zucchini,
    Go
        down—

In the most delightful way
See Coleman grow today
Happily he laughs and eats
While Mommy feeds at his feet

A spoonful of peaches
Makes the zucchini,
    Go
        down—

Zucches and peachinis
Mixed -- grows big boys from teeny
  Down—
    Down—
      Down—
          To the tummy
Where taste-good is found – yummy!

("Song" by Coleman's mother.)

A-Jumping and A-Growing

                    up
Gloria goes   and
                              down—
Happy all the while,
She says, "Watch me as I go
Look! See my great big smile!

Watch me! Here I come, Mommy.
See me, Daddy, too,
                    up
I go--   and
                              down
In my jump-a-roo.

                                        w
                                    o
                              r
                        g
Jumping and jumping – I
Happy in all I do,
Watch me, Mommy and Daddy—
In my jump-a-roo."

Ana Luisa

Ah! Little rosebud born before
Coming into full bloom—
Sweetly delicate and fragile
Leaving your mother's womb

Ah! Little rosebud so – so small;
July's sweet song you sang
Before this October began,
Early you felt earth's harsh pang

Ah! Little rosebud so precious—
'Twas your time to arrive,
Seemed too early to leave your warmth
We pray you grow and thrive

Ah! Little rosebud so wanted
Loving gift heaven sent—
We celebrate your arrival
A most blessed advent

Ah! Little rosebud you are loved
God in heaven knows you,
Prayers are lifted up for strength—
May you blossom anew.

vi.   *Journey with the wind*

...whispers from the heart

Quiet Meditation

Like beaded dew on purple iris petals
Found with the freshness of mornings' regal,
Thoughts come but ne'er seen; their message to impart
Are words whispered e'er so gently from the heart.

Does the dew talk to the iris while at rest?
Or, does the iris sing to the dew feeling blest?
It seems a simple enough question to ask
All being part of the life cycle with tasks

The simple beauty of the dew on iris;
How quietly they interrelate with no bias,
Often thoughts, as the morning dew, quickly part
Oft' before they can be whispered from the heart

Such simplicity found in God's creation
Existing within manmade complications;
The irises; the dew; the morning; the thoughts
Gentle whisperings from the heart – comfort brought

I Wish for You

I wish for you – as days go by
Bright sun – cloudless blue sky,
Warm gentle winds – but full of zest
Comfort with rest

I wish for you – silver nor gold
But needs met in household,
Grandchildren to follow your feet
Smiles from all you should meet

I wish for you – all happiness
Dreams realized and bliss,
Freedom to be one's self
While maintaining good health

I wish for you – productive days
Work challenge – creative ways,
Safety to home – freedom from wrath
Time to walk garden path

I wish for you – the peace within
Knowing where you have been,
Directions on how to proceed
To meet your ev'ry need

I wish for you – light from above
Pointing; guiding with love,
Faith in the Lord God ever strong
E'er knowing you belong

Today

Tomorrow is not yet
Yesterday is gone
Today is all we have
Dear Lord, lead us on

Play Practice

Pretty little girl dressing your doll
Putting on her sock and shoe
Enjoying your Christmas gift so small
Someday you're a Mommy, too

My Inner Athenaeum

Today I've learned more about myself
Some things that need placing on a shelf;
'Tis a hard thing to learn weaknesses
Especially, when in one's peakness.

Ah! One has to begin sometime
Glancing through the pages of life –
The bibliography began,
The complete summary remains

To be written – story conquered
As someone's mind has remembered
But, now I must reflect to see;
Can there be found any wisdom in me?

Decisions were made at key times
Not all were correct; made in blind;
Yet, prayerfully went on that way
Trying to do my best each day.

I can recapitulate
That which I recognize to date,
Years were not spent complacently
There my satisfaction would be

The self largely denied; the thoughts hid
One doesn't think – when others bid;
Life moves along through its stages—
One day one reflects on pages

Lackadaisical not my style
Creatively busy all the while;
Love's expression ne'er understood
Trying to do what e'er I could

Today I am reminiscent
About how former days were spent;
Page by page – place old on the shelf
Now, I shall learn about myself.

Life is incomprehensible
Sometimes it seems nonsensical,
Created for purpose there's no doubt
It just takes a lifetime to find out.

After thorough evaluation
Of my ev'ry situation,
I shall commence acting anew
Just as I am supposed to do

But, it's probable I will find
That deep within the soul of mine,
God in His infinite power
Made me as I am – for this hour.

Ah! My inner athenaeum
Reserved for only me to come;
I review; I reflect; I give praise
Page by page for all of my days.

On Paper with Pen

A single page upon which to write
From inside out come words to ignite,
A thought to remember or forget
A hurt to be healed or comfort let
So powerful is the pen in hand –
Moments' thoughts changed with written command.
The mind takes in what is felt when read
Thank you, Lord, for this light you've shed,
May I on the page write to uplift
And may I from this purpose not shift

Medical Clinic Exchange

Religious heritage to preserve
We came to Russia to serve
In all our ways, we acknowledge Him
Sometimes, seeing the world dim
Yet, clearly in our desire to work
From the task, we will not shirk

We give – the blood pressure checks
They give – some hugs around necks

We give – more blood sugar tests
They give – such sweet thoughts for rest

We give – the Doctor's treatments
They give – love-trust supplements

We give – medicines galore
They give – "Spacebos" and more

We give – so prayerfully
They give – apples picked from tree

The medical clinics worked by five
Great time to care, share, and be alive,
Orphanages served by three members
Made this a blessed trip to remember,
While our bodies may have become tired
Our hearts, dear Lord, forever inspired.

Taking the Midnight Train to Moscow
(Leaving Bryansk)

"Got my train – got my reservation"
Ticket in hand – am ready to go,
Clock hand near twelve at railway station
Taking the midnight train to Moscow

On board I have anticipation
Feeling the train move along the track,
Six hours crossing this great nation
Clickety-clack; on, clickety-clack

The sky so dark; stars shining bright
Trees pass by -- so quickly they do go,
Day dreamin' while a-travelin' tonight
Taking the midnight train to Moscow

Up in our berths with sleep a-comin'
Lulled by the gentle swayin' motion,
Hear those railroad cars a-hummin'
Rumblin' tw'rds home across the ocean

Satisfaction – our work is complete
Helpin' the people so they will know
God loves them and He will safely keep,
Taking the midnight train to Moscow.

The Melody

There's music deep within my heart
I hear the melody
The rhythm of my soul enthralls
Songs wanting to be free

Like a carousel – round and round
I hear the melody
Allowing myself to be as planned
Finding life's rhapsody

Thank you, Lord, for the melody
Life constantly changing
Thank you, Lord, for song in me
You are rearranging.

Morning Thoughts
(Sometimes, I Wonder)

My feelings like a stream run deep

Sometimes – I wonder if
This world is as vast
As the depths of my soul
I feel the fullness of the mass

Farther – than the arm can reach

Sometimes – I wonder if
Others ever feel as deep
To depths of the ocean
Or top of mountain so steep

Farther – than the eye can see

Sometimes – I wonder if
The sky can hold unfolding streams
With no openings to my feelings
Of my many thoughts and dreams

Farther still – through seamless seams
But close to God Supreme

Upstairs Window

Upstairs window looking at me
I wonder what you see
Firmly affixed there to your space
With brightness on your face

Do you see the green grass on ground?
With children all around
Playing their games and singing songs
Knowing where they belong

Upstairs window looking at me
Full view in sight by tree
Sheep in meadow – cattle grazing
Farmers their crops raising

Working in the hot sun of day
With rain coming their way
Coming and going of seasons
Living is their reason

Upstairs window – what do you hide
Behind curtains inside?
External reflections in sight
Until coming of night

Quiet darkness comes o'er all the earth
Window – then what's your worth?
Overseeing the blackness of hills
Ah! Heavens' light shines still.

The Gossamer Wing

Flimsily passing through this life
Managing all our strife
A cobweb of intricacies
Woven delicately

The softly veiled days seem unclear
Far away things so near
Dreams chased e'en after dulled focus
Goal 'tis diaphanous

Firmly striving to plan our way
Kind living day to day
Remembering cloudy gauze-like thoughts
Of path's direction sought

Ethereal melodies
Crossing the crystal sea
Life likened to gossamer wing
Without the Lord – nothing.

Two Ladies

Arriving at the Sizemore Cemetery
Wind carried melody
Bagpiper stood on high green knoll
Awesome sight to behold

The pipes droned the musical sound
Sweet reverence abound
Music to accompany walk
Up the hill; quiet; no talk

Family gathered – together
Comforting each other
'Twas sudden death of pair so dear
Burial service here

Ministers speaking in valley –
Prayer – Psalm 23
Serene beauty surrounded all
Sunshine; blue sky; peaceful

Devotions giv'n in beautiful way
On the October day
Sisters will rest on mountain hill
Souls released – bodies still

Flowers like a mountain garden—
Yellow, peach, lavender
Given to honor the women;
Final tribute – Amen.

Bagpiper began playing hymn;
Walking downhill in line—
Amazing Grace heard through the hills
Glory to God – hearts filled.

Times of Life

To everything there is a season
A time for every purpose –
Ecclesiastes writer reasons,
A summary of life at most

A time to be born
A time to die,
A time to plant
A time to reap comes nigh.
A time to kill
A time to heal,
A time to breakdown
A time to build up revealed.
A time to weep
A time to laugh – enhanced
A time to mourn
A time to dance
A time to cast away stones
A time to gather stones together,
A time to embrace
A time to refrain embracing each other
A time to get
A time to lose without delay,
A time to keep
A time to cast away,
A time to rend
A time to sew.
A time to keep silence
A time to speak – we know
A time to love
A time to hate.
A time of war
A time of peace – don't negate.

A season for everything
A purpose for every time,
I pray for deep understanding
Peace, joy and love to live sublime.

Wonder

Wonder 'tis the dance of the soul
Embrace as joy unfolds
Experience the melody
Marvel in rhapsody
Each day God's surprise – self enhances
Wonder – soul's awesome dance

Finding Quietness

To be near You, Lord
        I wandered in the church alone
            Looking for silence

Musical notes clang in the sanctuary
        The young pianist plays and
            The people talk trying to convince

I find a seat by a hallway window—
        People talk as the purple flowers bow;
            My wandering takes me outside

It is cool and damp. I sit.
        There are noises but happy sounds;
            The birds cheerfully confide

I listen and smile; happily I write—
        Lord, I wandered to be near You
            In quietness austere

When all the time;
        You had wandered with me—
            Quietly near.

vii.   *Journey with the wind*

...within the shadowed valleys

Fragility

Lo! We are all travelers
From beginning eternity
To eternity we go;
Walking sometimes in pity

We creep; we walk; we run so
As winds blow and the tides roll
We move along our way
Travelers with weary souls

Noise of lifetime; peace of mind
Come and go throughout our life
Confusion bewilders and blinds
Travelers facing such strife

Yet, looking through human eyes
There is beauty in flowers
In the fragile existence
We, travelers, share this hour

Lo! We are all travelers
With great opportunities –
As vast as the burdens shared;
Delicate jewels we can be.

"The Pain of Looking So Good"
A Plea From Those With a Chronic Irreversible Disease

"You sure do look good,"
We hear the people say.
The intended encouragement
Has a very negative way.

Dear friends, there is little comfort
In "looking good" outside
When horrible continuous muscle aches
Within the body abide.

The fatigue is overwhelming
Yet, we try out best to go.
When we are told how good we look
Our verbal response is slow.

If we look so good
Then, our pain must not be real.
If we look so good
Then, our fatigue must not be as we feel.

Dear friends, the pain and fatigue are real –
Whether from treatment or disease.
So, when you pass us by
A nice smile and "hello" will please.

We are glad we look good; however,
Please spare us anguish
In hearing about our physical appearance,
Just thank God for our presence.

Compassion E'er We Sleep

We need to wake before we die
Do we have compassion?
Do we care where some others lie?
Is there any passion?

Ah! But tiredness does prevail
It is easy not to care,
Or, complacent – world by the tail
Perhaps, we want not to share.

Arteries of compassion clogged
Is that the way life takes?
Going through life completely fogged
Until dying to wake?

We have wealth with failure to see
That sensitivity,
Compassion and encouragement
Gives to one's life beauty

With glimpses of eternity –
Heaven is real – God-sent.
At the gate, we know compassion
With encouragement

'Tis the way to show love.
A friend needs to see traits,
Displayed action through Christ above,
Before one's life abates.

May I reach out to those I should?
Oh! Lord! I humbly pray
Compassion to give for the good
Helping someone today.

Thinking About Life's Struggles and Rewards

I think about the small wild rose
Trying to bloom amid the thorns
And how the brush is all around
Hindering the rose being born.

I think about the child who tries
To learn to walk with crooked feet
And how the services to correct
Are tangled – attempts incomplete

I think about the noble elder
Trying to remain in his home
Only to find it difficult
To be heard; thus, left all alone

I think of the growing green grass
Trying to grow without moisture
Beginning to wither and fade
Awaiting the rain to come pure

I think of farmers hard at work
Mowing, plowing, trying to reap
In all seasons and at all times
Providing for family's keep

I think of retirees who stopped
Using their creativity;
Despondent with little purpose
Or, so it seems – a used to be

I think of the birds singing songs
Their melody fills the morning
They work to build their nest for new
Continually adorning

Oh! To be as the birds of air
Flittering to and from with care
Having all needs met with the simplest;
God in His goodness always there

The rose breaks bondage with sweetness;
While the child learns to walk in love;
The aged person perseveres
As does the grass with rain above

Ah! The birds bring such contentment
In feathery simplicity;
Placing in gentle perspective,
God, in love, brings felicity

Purpose can be gained throughout life
By weeding out decades of thorns,
When purpose is looked for and found –
New hopes; new dreams; new lives are born.

Quagmire of Desolation

The mind of man 'tis out of view
Holding years upon years
Thoughts-words-hurts-feelings that somehow
Build up – fail to bring tears

Oh! To be able to reach in
Pull hurts out one by one
Disappointments abuse sorrow
All collected undone

Then in life; a critical time
Resolution not met –
Darkness overtakes the brightness
Insanity is set

Temporary confusion dwells
Emotions overwhelmed
Hurt so intense – unable to talk
Real person gone from helm

Like a boat lost at sea – floating
Until barrier hit and then –
Forward movement or stuck in mire
Not knowing where or when

Happened so quickly – actions rash;
One's life is taken in a flash –

******

To end one's life before God's time
Such a mystery;
Especially a child of God
And, forever will be.

A Prayerful Thought

The morning clouds hang heavy
It seems they're in a bevy –
Not separated by light
Just the color of graphite

This is the day the Lord made
Acknowledgment does not fade;
Yet, the sky is enclosed gray
Lord, help all get through this day

Ah! The clouds have rolled away
A new perspective holds sway;
Nothing so dreary a day brings
When the Master handles things.

Triumphant Core

Inside the inside is me –
The height of tranquility
Like a river flows peacefully
Yet, appears transparency
A complex duality

Inside the inside is me –
Deeper still – complexities
Sorrows lie reluctantly;
Camouflaged intricacies
Remaining uncertainties

Inside the inside is me –
Made so very wondrously
Like rose in bloom so lovely;
With roots worn gradually –
My inside shall always be

Inside the inside is me –
Unlike pearls floating on sea
Assurance held preciously;
My soul secure completely
Never e'er precariously

Outside the outside of me –
Will lie in dark earth crusty,
As the world twirls cautiously
So serendipitously –
Yet, hungry and with worry

Inside the inside of me,
Complete through eternity –
As I cross the crystal sea,
Robed in perfect harmony;
I'll dwell in His majesty.